MacFarlane, Lang & Co 'Pansy', 1929, length 26 cm. 'Walnut', 1927, length 26 cm. (This was the first in a series of four tins. It is, however, the only one not to be named after the flowers on the lid. Instead, it is named after the background 'wood' effect.) 'Rose', 1931, length 26 cm.

BISCUIT TINS

Tracy Dolphin

The Shire Book

Published in 1999 by Shire Publications Ltd,
Cromwell House, Church Street, Princes Risborough,
Buckinghamshire HP27 9AA, UK.
(Website www.shirebooks.co.uk)

Copyright © 1999 by Tracy Dolphin.
First published 1999.
ISBN 0 7478 0425 7
Tracy Dolphin is hereby identified as the author of this
work in accordance with Section 77 of the Copyright,
Designs and Patents Act 1988.

British Library Cataloguing in Publication Data:
Dolphin, Tracy
Biscuit tins. – (The Shire book)
1. Advertising tins – History
2. Advertising tins – Collectors and collecting
3. Tin containers – History
4. Tin containers – Collectors and collecting
I. Title 739.5'32
ISBN 0 7478 0425 7

Printed in Great Britain by CIT Printing Services Ltd,
Press Buildings, Merlins Bridge, Haverfordwest,
Pembrokeshire SA61 1XF.

Note on the captions: if a tin has an accepted name or the name of the tin is known, this appears in quotation marks. Where a name is given without these marks, it is not the generally accepted name of the tin. All sizes given are approximate.

Cover: *(Left-hand row, from the front) McVitie & Price sample tin c.1905; Macfarlane, Lang & Co 'Lady's Bag', 1909; Huntley & Palmers 'Money Box', 1933. (Centre, from the front) William Crawford & Sons 'Rich Tea' sample, c.1935; Huntley & Palmers 'Arabesque', 1893; Carr & Co 'Cheese Assorted' tin, c.1952. (On top of this; clockwise from front left) McVitie & Price sample tin, c.1926; Macfarlane, Lang & Co 'Granola' tube, 1930s; Carr & Co 'Nursery Rhymes', 1895; Huntley & Palmers Superior Reading Biscuits, c.1933. (Right-hand row, from the front) W. & R. Jacob 'Cream Cracker' sample, c.1930; CWS 'Books', c.1913; Huntley & Palmers 'Lantern', 1911.*

ACKNOWLEDGEMENTS
I would like to thank the following people for their help with this book: Michael Bott at the University of Reading and Javier Pes at Reading Museum. Also Richard and Celia Cotton, Karin Hughes, Cliff Dolphin, Henry Jaremko, Brian Screaton and Liz McClair. All photographs are copyright Tracy Dolphin, except those on pages 17 and 29 (centre), which are copyright Reading Museum (Reading Borough Council). All rights reserved.

Contents

The biscuit companies

Sweet biscuits were developed in the early nineteenth century. Their predecessors, tack or ship's biscuits, had been used for several centuries as rations on board ship. There were many biscuit companies in Britain in the nineteenth and early twentieth centuries. Some were national concerns, but most were local companies that supplied a small area of the country. Fortt's of Bath were one of the latter; they invented the Bath Oliver biscuit, which was soon copied by most of the national companies. Biscuit production began on a small scale. Local bakers supplied their own town or village with a product that was sold loose or in paper bags and would be eaten within a day or two of purchase. For this type of business word of mouth was sufficient to generate adequate sales, but urbanisation caused an interruption in the passing on of family knowledge, hence the rise of advertising to fill the gap.

The development of branded goods and advertising are inseparable and are attributable to the growth of road and rail communications in the first half of the nineteenth century, and to developments in the printing industry. Also food adulteration scares caused the public to turn towards companies that could be held accountable. Distribution of biscuits on a national scale demanded packaging that would protect the products from softening by exposure to air and from breakage by rough handling. Tin boxes provided the solution to this need.

Huntley & Palmers of Reading were by far the largest biscuit manufacturer by the late nineteenth century. In the 1830s they arranged for their biscuits to be sold at a coaching inn near their premises, which meant that they became known to customers from all over the country, soon leading to the need for national distribution. They pioneered the use of decorated biscuit tins as a marketing aid in the 1860s and over the years produced the largest number of tin boxes. Huntley & Palmers became so well known that they passed into folklore, with the saying 'that takes the biscuit' becoming 'that takes the Huntley & Palmers'. In 1921 they joined with Peek, Frean & Co to set up Associated Biscuits.

CWS 'Biscuits', c.1900. One of the few early tins to show biscuits in the design. (Length 25.5 cm)

Palmer Brothers 'Work Basket', c.1898, length 13 cm. Marsh & Co 'Basket', c.1900, length 16 cm; 'Wallet'; c.1905, width 13 cm.

This was an umbrella company used mainly to secure better buying power of raw materials. They were taken over by Nabisco Brands in 1962 and ceased trading in the late 1980s.

Carr & Co of Carlisle was established in 1831 by Jonathan Dodgson Carr. In ten years he expanded his business to the point where he was the first biscuit manufacturer to be issued with a royal warrant. In the 1840s he introduced the first biscuit-cutting machine; this increased supply and led to further mechanisation within the industry. His sons and grandsons also invented new biscuits and machines for making them. In 1972 United Biscuits bought the company but they continue to

Huntley & Palmers' Christmas tin list, 1900.

Early designs for paper labels: Huntley & Palmers' Factory, designed in 1876, this example c.1930, length 22 cm. Carr & Co standard label designed in the 1880s, this example c.1905, length 22 cm.

trade under their own name.

W. & R. Jacob & Co originated in Dublin; they began making sweet biscuits in 1851. Expansion of sales into England prompted them to establish a factory in Liverpool in 1914; this was fortunate because after the creation of the Irish Free State in 1922 there had to be separate companies for Britain and Ireland. In 1960 they joined Associated Biscuits, which in turn became Nabisco Brands. In 1989 they became Jacob's Bakery Group.

The Co-operative Wholesale Society (CWS) has its roots in Lancashire in the 1840s. It was not solely a biscuit manufacturer but made all manner of food and goods for working-class communities. The appeal

Carr & Co 'Hunting', c.1900, length 16 cm; 'Lakes', 1892, length 16 cm; 'The Original Biscuit Factory', c.1906, length 15 cm.

W. & R. Jacob & Co 'British Empire Exhibition, Wembley', 1924, diameter 7 cm; 'Miniature Tin', 1929, height 7.5 cm.

and success of the co-operative shops lay in the issuing of dividends based on the total amount of money spent in a shop over a fixed period. The wholesale department was established in 1863 to supply goods to extant shops. The first factory was established in 1873 in Crumpsall, north of Manchester, to make biscuits. Amalgamation of the individual retail and wholesale societies, and a dividend system the same as that on the retail side of the business, made it the largest wholesaler in Britain at the turn of the century. By the beginning of the Second World War the CWS was supplying 23 per cent of groceries in the United Kingdom. The company still has a major high street presence today.

MacFarlane, Lang & Co began trading in Glasgow in 1817 as bakers. It was not until 1886 that they began to make biscuits. By 1903 it became necessary to open another factory in Fulham in London. In 1948 they formed United Biscuits with McVitie & Price. Today most of their biscuits have been taken over by the McVitie's label.

William Crawford began business in Edinburgh in 1813 and is the oldest biscuit manufacturer in Britain. In 1897 a new factory was established at Liverpool, which was incorporated into the main business in 1900. They covered the whole country with a policy of having 'a customer in every street or road who could pay and buy'. Deliveries were dispatched within two days of the order being taken, which established them as a reliable manufacturer. The 1930s were the high point of their business. In 1962 Crawford's joined MacFarlane, Lang and McVitie & Price at United Biscuits.

Peek, Frean & Co was established in 1857. After a shaky beginning the company went from strength to strength owing to a healthy export policy. Strong links with France and the United States of America are evident in the style of the company's advertising and tin-box decoration. Their revolutionary Pearl biscuit of 1865 was the precursor of all modern biscuit varieties. By 1914 Peek, Frean were one of the largest manufacturers and after the First World War joined with Huntley & Palmers in forming Associated Biscuits. Their products are still available today.

McVitie's are probably the best-known biscuit manufacturer today. They began business in 1809 as bakers in Edinburgh. In 1888 Charles

Left: *CWS Mistletoe, c.1910, width 21 cm; 'Anemones', 1920s, width 16 cm: this tin was made in several different sizes; 'Factory at Crumpsall', c.1906, width 12 cm.*

Below: *William Crawford & Sons sample tins: Delft, c.1935, length 27 cm; Venice, c.1933, length 27 cm; Parrot, c.1936, length 19.5 cm; Flowers, c.1937, length 18 cm.*

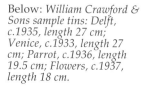
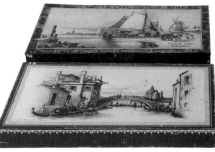

Below: *Peek, Frean & Co Christmas tin list, 1908.*

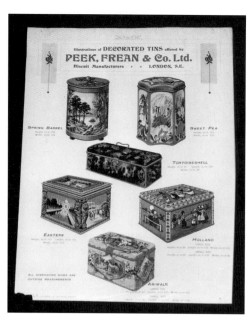

Price, a traveller with Cadbury's, joined the firm. His sales and promotions boosted the company profile and he became a partner. McVitie & Price were innovators in marketing, being one of the most aggressive sellers to the trade. Consequently they expanded rapidly in the first decade of the twentieth century. After the Second World War a series of mergers formed United Biscuits, and since about 1970 most of the products made by the other companies have acquired the McVitie's label.

These are the most significant companies of the nineteenth and early twentieth centuries. Other companies that produced tins during this period are: Meredith & Drew of London; Gray, Dunn of Glasgow; Marsh & Co of Belfast; the A1 Biscuit Company, Battersea; Henderson's of Edinburgh; Wright's of South Shields; R. Middlemass & Son, Edinburgh; Palmer Brothers of Bristol; Dunmore's of South Wigston; George

Left: *McVitie & Price 'Stork', 1938, diameter 11 cm: this sold for two shillings; paper-labelled sample tin, c.1905, width 13 cm; 'George V Silver Jubilee' sample tin, 1935, width 12 cm.*

Right: *R. Middlemass & Son 'Dragonfly', c.1911, width 20 cm: this 'tin' is made of oxidised copper plate. W. Dunmore & Son 'The Old Story', c.1902, width 17 cm. Peak, Frean & Co 'Primrose', 1906, 12 cm square.*

Kemp, Cardiff; and MacKenzie & MacKenzie, Edinburgh.

After the Second World War there was a significant change in the biscuit industry. Mergers and marketing plans altered the names of the most successful companies. Burton's, formerly a supplier of raw materials to the biscuit manufacturers, began to make their own biscuits and cakes. Fox's, established in 1853, started to dominate the market in the 1980s. American take-overs gave Nabisco prominence in the 1950s and 1960s. Elkes, Kemp's and Parkinson's all enjoyed a brief success in the post-war era. Companies that had never made biscuits before expanded into the market, such as the Mazawattee Tea Company. Today chocolate manufacturers such as Cadbury's and own name brands such as Marks & Spencer all vie for a slice of the market. McVitie's are still the market leaders in Britain.

Below: *Frear's Seagull by C. F. Tunnicliffe, 1956, width 28 cm. Elkes Biscuits Circus, c.1955, width 20 cm.*

Tinplate

Technological advances and a larger communications network enabled shop-bought biscuits to be consumed by a wider, mainly middle-class, public. The main stumbling block in supplying the expanding market was transportation, as the biscuits quickly became soft if they were exposed to the open air for extended periods. Biscuits on board ships were usually kept in wooden barrels, but these were subject to wood-worm and damp. Tinplate was an obvious solution to the problem. It was robust but not heavy, and it could be given an airtight seal, thereby preventing the biscuits from becoming soft. Also containers could be made in standard sizes. Production of tinplate had begun in Pontypool in the late 1600s, and all manner of household goods (tinware) were manufactured. Tinplate in the early nineteenth century was made of iron coated with tin (nowadays, steel coated with tin). John Walker, a matchmaker in Stockton-on-Tees, and Thomas Huntley, a biscuit baker in Reading, were the first to use tin boxes as a method of keeping their goods dry. Thomas Huntley's were made by his brother Joseph, who founded Huntley, Boorne & Stevens.

These early tins were made by hand and cut from standard-sized sheets of tinplate weighing 115 pounds (52.2 kg). A trained box maker could make about a hundred per day and it was not long before de-mand outstripped supply. Lithographed or 'enamelled' tins were issued for the Christmas market. The early tins from the late 1860s and 1870s were simple in shape because the transfer decoration was tricky to apply accurately, but by the 1890s shapes had become much more complicated with often as many as twenty or thirty pieces per tin, all of which were assembled by hand. This trend continued up to the First World War. In the 1920s and 1930s increased mechanisation and higher wages led to tins that were much simpler in shape and design, and this trend has continued to the present day.

Huntley & Palmers 'Shakespeare', 1912, height 18 cm; 'Japanese', 1908, height 15.5 cm: the shape of this tin was first used in 1893–5.

The tin-box manufacturers

Tin boxes were very useful for products that needed to be kept dry such as biscuits, mustard, tobacco and tea. But tinplate was more than just a useful packaging material: lithographic decoration techniques made tin boxes highly desirable products in themselves, and many items were sold in tin packaging when it was not necessary – for example corsets and dress shields, make-up, pills and nails. There were many manufacturers of tin boxes and cans active in the last half of the nineteenth century. Those mainly associated with the biscuit trade were Huntley, Boorne & Stevens; Barringer, Wallis & Manners; and Hudson Scott & Sons, though they all made boxes for other types of companies.

Huntley, Boorne & Stevens began supplying boxes to Huntley & Palmer of Reading in the 1840s. By 1863 they were supplying hinged tins with all-over paper labels for shop display. They were the first company to combine tin box making with the printing of tin sheets. Steam presses were introduced in 1871 and machines for stamping out the printed tinplate came into use in 1875. Also in 1875, they were licensed by Bryant & May, the matchmakers, to print designs on the tinplate by offset lithography (see page 14) and led the way in tin-box decoration up to the expiry of the patents in 1889. They continued to expand and remained independent until 1918, when they were bought by Huntley & Palmers.

Barringer, Wallis & Manners began as Barringer & Brown, packers of mustard. By the 1860s they had begun to sell mustard in tins. These were handmade by their own workers from tin sheets decorated by the Tin Plate Decorating Company of Wales. In the 1880s designs on tinplate

Three tins made by Huntley, Boorne & Stevens. Huntley & Palmers 'Lantern', 1911, height 23 cm; 'Marble', 1909, height 18 cm; 'Sentries', 1914, height 17.5 cm. A tin made by Hudson Scott & Sons for CWS, 'Carnation Glove Box', 1910, length 26 cm.

Tin-box manufacturers' catalogues: Barringer, Wallis & Manners Ltd, 1927; Hudson Scott & Sons Ltd, 1911, showing 'Blue Bird', which was bought by McVitie & Price in 1911 and CWS in 1912.

were bought from White & Pike, lithographic printers, of Birmingham. The two companies formed a partnership whereby White & Pike obtained orders for tin boxes and decorated the tinplate, and Barringer's made up the plate into boxes. In 1890 Charles Manners became the managing director of the company and developed the box-making side of the business further. By 1892 relations with White & Pike had deteriorated. Barringer's therefore decided to move into the decorating side of the business, to which end they employed James Kirkbride of Hudson Scott & Sons to be in charge of the printing department and took on their first artists. In 1893 their first offset lithography machine was bought, although at this time they still bought in a lot of the artwork. In 1895 they became a limited company and severed connections with the mustard-packing business. By 1896 they were taking on representatives to sell their designs to trade customers. All their representatives opened new accounts within weeks of setting out on the road. In 1903 they installed the first rotary press in Britain, which speeded up production, making them one of the leading manufacturers of tin boxes. They were bought by Metal Box in 1939.

Hudson Scott & Sons of Carlisle began business as paper printers in 1799. They began transfer-printing tin sheets in 1876. These were supplied to Carr's, the biscuit manufacturers, and others, for making up into boxes. In 1886 they began to make the boxes too. They used a process imported from France by H. E. V. Baber, which seems to have been in legal competition with the patents held by Huntley, Boorne & Stevens. However, it was not contested. They made tins for Carr's and Peek, Frean, as well as advertising plaques in tin and advertisements in card and paper. Jacob's had had business dealings with them since 1855. In 1889, when the offset patents expired, Hudson Scott were in a good position to capture a large part of the market. From an early date, their work was renowned for its fine quality as they were able to number several well-known artists among their staff, such as John Bushby and Paul Greville Hudson. Hudson Scott also supplied tin boxes to Queen Victoria in 1899, thereby obtaining a royal warrant. They formed Metal Box with Barclay & Fry and several smaller companies in 1922.

Tins made by Hudson Scott & Sons: CWS 'Factory at Crumpsall', c.1900, width 14 cm; Peek, Frean & Co 'Hamper', c.1902, width 8.5 cm: this was also issued by John Hill & Sons in 1903.

Decoration

Moiré métallique was a favoured method of decorating tinplate in the 1840s and 1850s. This technique gave an all over 'crackled' effect, caused by the tinplate being heated, treated with nitro-muriatic acid and then painted or varnished, leaving a crystalline decoration.

Embossing was a permanent way of identifying the manufacturer and contents and has been used continuously since the 1830s. It was later used as a means of highlighting the surface design of lithographed tins.

Stencilling names and designs was also used but did not produce a permanent decoration owing to the intractability of tin.

Lithographic printing on paper was a cheap way of mass-producing coloured artwork and from the 1820s was increasingly used in commercial work. By the 1840s a small paper label depicting 'Huntley & Palmers Biscuit Manufactory' was in use, printed by a company in London. A description of Carr's labels at this time is quoted from the *Handbook to the Lancaster and Carlisle Railway* published in 1847: 'packed in neat tin boxes of three and five pounds, labelled with an engraving of the city of Carlisle, the royal arms and the maker's name'.

Lithography, or printing, on tinplate was developed in the 1860s and became the primary method of decorating tins; it is still used today. There are several types of printing used in tin-box manufacture.

Direct printing was a method whereby the ink was printed directly on to the tin by means of a lithographic stone. This often meant that the ink did not stick very well, as there was no absorbency between the two materials. Direct printing often involved only two colours,

Huntley & Palmers 'Worcester' , 1912, height 22 cm. MacFarlane, Lang & Co 'Romney', 1907, height 18 cm. Peak, Frean & Co 'Horseshoe', 1900, width 14 cm. Huntley & Palmers 'Needlework', 1930, width 15 cm.

Upper left: *The biscuit companies' names were often embossed on to the bottom of the tin: Peek Frean & Co 'Arabian', 1897; CWS 'Books', c.1913.*

Lower left: *Direct printing: early 'Neath' tin made by The Tin Plate Decorating Co, c.1875, width 18 cm. The gold effect is 'moiré metallique' with a black overlay. Huntley, Boorne & Stevens made 'Travellers' for Huntley & Palmers. Although the design looks as though it has been applied by direct printing, the tin is marked 'B & Ms Pat', which means it has been applied by offset lithography. The handles can differ. Before 1889, length 34.5 cm.*

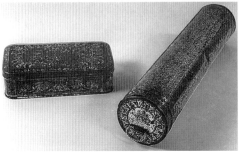

frequently black on a gold ground. (For some time it was thought that Huntley & Palmers 'Travellers' was printed by this method but it was actually printed by the offset method as it is marked 'B & Ms Pat' (Bryant & May's patent).

In the 1860s transfer printing was developed, which was a method similar to that used in the potteries. The picture was printed on porous, gummed paper; the colours were applied in reverse so that the transparent colours were put on first and the opaque colours last. The tinplate was coated with a transparent varnish and when it was almost dry the transfer was applied and pressed on an iron bed. When the transfer and varnish were dry the tinplate was soaked to remove the paper, and the gum was removed with a sponge. Then it was baked in an oven, varnished and baked again. In this and later processes the tinplate was printed flat and then shaped into the boxes by hand on a triangular shaped mandril, the designs incorporated black lines to show the box maker where to make the bends. By 1900 dies were being used to stamp out the shape.

In 1875 Robert Barclay and John Doyle Fry registered two patents for offset lithography. This method employed a glazed cardboard (later rubber) 'blanket' which acted as a buffer between the lithographic stone and metal plate. The design from the stone was printed on to the cardboard, which was immediately 'offset' on to the tinplate. This is sometimes rather confusingly called the 'direct' method. Barclay sold the rights of this process to Bryant & May, who in turn licensed Huntley, Boorne & Stevens as sole manufacturer. The patents lasted until 1889, whereupon other manufacturers could produce tins by this method.

Photolithography was first used in the mid 1920s. Photographic plates made the decorating process much quicker; the skills of the lithographic artist were no longer needed, and the stippled effect which was the 'trademark' of offset lithography became a thing of the past.

Offset lithography: Huntley & Palmers 'Gypsy', 1893, height 15 cm; 'Arabian Nights', 1894, height 15 cm: two of a series of four; 'Arabesque', 1893, length 21.5 cm.

Peek, Frean & Co trade stand at the International Health Exhibition, London, 1884.

Shop display

By the end of the nineteenth century cellophane wrappers had been introduced for biscuits for everyday consumption. These were usually penny packets or half a pound (228 grams) by weight. Other types of wrapping used in the first half of the twentieth century included waxed tubes and greased paper. Owing to their flimsiness these packets of

Left: *Huntley & Palmers 'Ginger Nuts' tin: the thin metal seal is still in place – it was opened by cutting along the edge with a knife, c.1930, length 22 cm. Waxed card tube, c.1934, height 20 cm. Sample of 'Currant Puffs', c.1900, width 11 cm: this tin has the remains of another type of airtight seal. Metal seals were particularly useful for tins sent to hot climates.*

Right: *Shop display: (Top) Carr & Co 2 ³/₄ pound (1.25 kg) 'Cheese Assorted' tin with labels designed in the 1880s and 1900s, c.1952, width 23 cm. (Left) Huntley & Palmers 7 pound (3.18 kg) 'Petit Beurre' tin with glass lid, 1950s, height 27 cm. (Right) Wyllie, Barr & Ross 7 pound (3.18 kg) 'British Wafer' tin, 1930s, height 24 cm. (Front) W. & R. Jacob & Co counter tin with glass lid, 1920s, height 12.5 cm; small counter tin with glass lid, c.1910, width 18.5 cm.*

15

Paper-labelled tins: W. & R. Jacob & Co 'Plasmon Biscuits', c.1912, width 17 cm; Peek, Frean & Co 'Swiss Cream Biscuits', c.1900, width 17.5 cm; William Crawford & Sons 'Bonnie Mary Shortbread' sample tin, c.1920, width 15.5 cm; Huntley & Palmers sample of 'Currant Puffs', c.1900, width 11 cm. Paper-labelled tins often have advertisements on the bottom; it is a useful way of dating them.

Paper-labelled tins: Huntley & Palmers 'Tea Rusks', c.1925, length 22 cm, decorated in the manner of the Beggarstaff Brothers who designed many advertising posters in the first quarter of the twentieth century; 'Afternoon Tea Biscuits', c.1926, length 26.5 cm; 'Chocolate Bridge Biscuits', c.1935, length 23 cm.

biscuits were transported in and sold from large tins that were covered in paper labels or inserted into wooden cabinets made specially to hold them. Paper-labelled tins could have different types of seal. Some were given a soldered inner lid; others had a piece of greaseproof paper glued on to the inner rim and then the outside paper labels were stuck down in one piece so that to open the tin it was necessary to cut through the paper.

Tins for use in shops came in many different sizes and shapes. The largest were approximately 9 pounds (4 kg) in weight, depending on the type of biscuit, and were often used to sell loose biscuits; the smallest were usually about half a pound (228 grams).

Paper labels for Huntley & Palmers tins, 1920s.

Paper-label designs were used for a long time. Some were the company's trademark, such as Huntley and Palmers' Garter and Buckle design created in 1851 or their 'factory' paper label, which was designed in 1876 and was still in use in the 1960s. Some were used for the lifetime of the biscuit, which could vary considerably. Others reflected the fashions of the time and were quickly replaced.

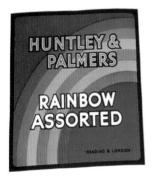

*Huntley &
Palmers: four
'Speciality' tins,
c.1870–80, length
15.5 cm. Specific
names were not
given to tins at this
time. Names
usually referred to
the biscuits inside.*

Tins 1868–1918

The first Christmas tins were usually rectangular with sharp or rounded corners and were mostly decorated by transfer printing or *moiré métallique*. Some of them had cardboard pictures stuck on the lid. Huntley & Palmers led the field; their early tins often had the company name on the sides or corners as part of the design. To start with there were only a few basic shapes, which were intricately decorated with flowers, shields, coats of arms and abstract designs in various colourways. Today these are usually called 'court' or 'speciality' tins although at the time they did not have names. Peek, Frean & Co were also issuing tins at this time; a description from a handbill of 1876 states: 'Cabinet. – A special assortment of 20 varieties, very choice; packed in a highly ornamented oval tin, forming an elegant Biscuit Box for the Table, with Book-mark Almanack enclosed. *(Special Show Card.) Tins not returnable.'* This was their only lithographed tin produced that year; several others were available with paper wrappers.

Decorating by offset lithography was developed during the 1870s. Huntley, Boorne & Stevens of Reading held the patents on this method until 1889; tins made by them before this date were marked 'B & Ms Pat' (Bryant & May's patent). This technique enabled more intricate designs and shapes to be used as the patterns could be placed more accurately on the tin sheet. The shapes were still based on a rectangle but were becoming more intricate with curved sides, domed lids and fancy shaped corners. More colours were used in the pictures, and these were laid down in a particular order: buff, yellow, pink, light blue, light grey, red, dark blue, brown, black and dark grey for shading. The depth of colour depended upon stippling the lithographic stone – the more dots added to the stone's surface, the darker the colour would be. Varnishes were also developed at the same time, with varying degrees of gloss, eggshell and rippled or crystalline effects.

*Huntley & Palmers:
(Back) 'Hunting',
1888, width 16.5
cm; 'Orient', 1887,
length 24 cm: this
tin was designed to
promote Huntley &
Palmers' new
Orient biscuits;
(front) 'Wild
Flowers', 1888,
width 18 cm: this
shape was used
extensively
throughout the
1880s and 1890s;
'Festal', 1888,
length 21 cm: this
name refers to the
biscuit selection
inside.*

There were several considerations that could contribute to the price of the tin: complexity of shape, cost of the artwork, types of hinges, soldered or folded seams, decorated bottoms and extras such as catches or locks and keys. In addition, the cost of the biscuits themselves, paper wrappings, calendars and scraps or collectable trade cards all had to be taken into account.

The cost of designing new shapes for tin boxes was the most expensive part of the design process, and early on Huntley & Palmers began making series of tins of the same shape but with different pictures. In a few cases the shape and decoration were the same, with the colour being the only difference. If a design was thought particularly good it was registered at the Patent Office and given a registered design number.

The tins were advertised to the trade by means of illustrated leaflets which showed them and described new varieties of biscuits. Grocers were also supplied with show cards and handbills, free samples to give away and larger tins of samples for the customer to try in the shop. Chemically preserved biscuits were supplied in flat, glass-fronted tins that were usually displayed on the wall. There were tin signs, and

*Huntley & Palmers
'Mexican', 1895,
width 16.5 cm;
'Harmony', 1893,
width 16.5 cm. Two
of a series.*

18

Carr & Co Christmas tin list 1892–3.

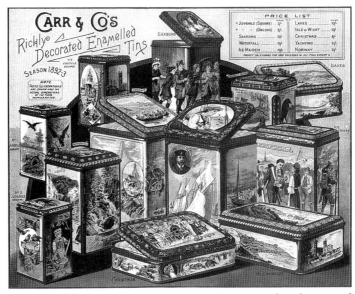

various novelties appeared, such as gramophone records, ashtrays and stationery.

The subject matter depicted on the tins of the 1880s and 1890s varied enormously. Subjects as diverse as gymkhanas and fairy tales were illustrated. Recurring themes included foreign countries and aspects of their cultures. Historical scenes, children's subjects, animals and the natural world were also continually popular.

The intricacy of the shapes reached a peak in the mid 1890s when a new type of tin emerged, shaped as a specific object. This began in about 1895 with a sequence of baskets and continued until 1914. The diversity of these objects was considerable. Sundials, lanterns, books, writing boxes and piles of plates all made an appearance. Some were designed to be used for a particular purpose after the biscuits had been consumed. Long oblong tins were often described as glove boxes; square tins were intended as handkerchief boxes. Art Nouveau styles became

Peek, Frean & Co 'Arabian', 1897, height 12 cm. Huntley & Palmers 'Arctic', 1897, diameter 12.5 cm. CWS 'Isle of Man', c.1890, height 14 cm

Huntley & Palmers 'Coach and Horses', 1888, width 16 cm; 'Albion', 1887, height 14.5 cm.

Huntley & Palmers 'With Dog and Gun', 1899. The stippled effect of offset lithography can be seen here, as can the fine embossing techniques used on the simpler shaped tins.

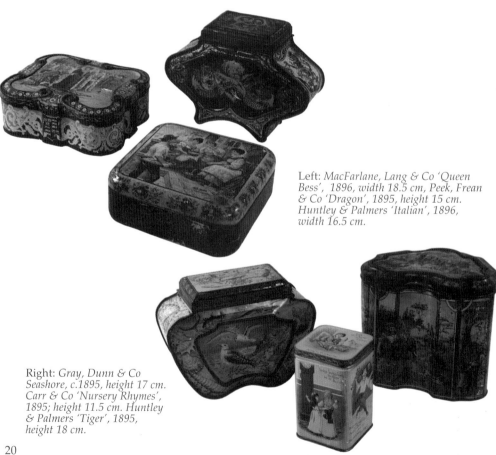

Left: MacFarlane, Lang & Co 'Queen Bess', 1896, width 18.5 cm, Peek, Frean & Co 'Dragon', 1895, height 15 cm. Huntley & Palmers 'Italian', 1896, width 16.5 cm.

Right: Gray, Dunn & Co Seashore, c.1895, height 17 cm. Carr & Co 'Nursery Rhymes', 1895; height 11.5 cm. Huntley & Palmers 'Tiger', 1895, height 18 cm.

(Left) Huntley & Palmers 'Log', 1902, width 18 cm; (Front) 'Wallet', 1903, width 18 cm; both have the patented catch. (Back) CWS 'Bag', c.1908, width 16 cm. (Right) A1 Biscuit Company 'Straw Basket', c.1895, width 15.5 cm.

Left: CWS Cherries c.1910, length 25.5 cm; 'Arcadian', c.1910, length 25.5 cm. Peek, Frean & Co 'Vineyard', 1903, length 25 cm.

Right: CWS 'Books', c.1913, width 11.5 cm. Huntley & Palmers 'Bookstand', 1905, height 16cm.

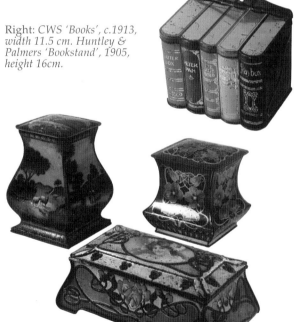

Gray, Dunn & Co Landscapes, c.1904, height 16.5 cm. Peek, Frean & Co 'Nasturtium', 1903, height 13 cm. W. & R. Jacob Art Nouveau Casket, c.1907, length 23.5 cm.

Huntley & Palmers 'Reticule', 1905, width 20.5 cm; 'Satchel', 1908, width 16 cm. Carr & Co 'Kit Bag', 1902, width 12.5 cm. All have handles made of tin. (Front) Huntley & Palmers 'Red Wallet', 1914–15, width 14 cm: the handle is made of coloured cord.

more common after about 1903. The intricate shape of these tins, which had little to do with the protection of the biscuits, necessitated protection of their own. All the special Christmas tins of this period, and probably from the 1880s and 1890s as well, had their own protective boxes or wrappers.

During the period from 1900 to 1914 'tin' boxes were made of other materials. Silver and copper oxides were used for surface decoration, and plain tins were given wickerwork or cloth-covered wooden shells. Some had mirrors in the lid. Sales of these intricate and delightful tins

Peek, Frean & Co 'Peacock', 1906, length 24.5 cm. Huntley & Palmers 'Cyprus', 1905, width 19.5 cm, decorated in imitation of copper and bronze; 'Poppies', 1912, width 16.5 cm; this was decorated to imitate painted, tooled leather.

Huntley & Palmers 'Silhouette', 1914, height 18 cm. MacFarlane, Lang & Co 'Carnation Biscuit Box', 1905, height 17 cm (including handle). Huntley & Palmers 'Egyptian', 1910, width 24.5 cm.

were high throughout this time. Tens of thousands of each design were made and sold at sixpence, a shilling, two shillings and three shillings and sixpence. These prices remained constant throughout the period. Huntley & Palmers' 'Roses' and 'Waterlilies', both issued in 1909, sold for two shillings each. The 'Sentry Box' of 1909 was a sixpenny tin. Some tins sold out in just one year; others were offered again over consecutive years until they were all sold. Some were so popular that they were reissued over a considerable period of time. The tins were advertised to the trade and the public in the editorial sections of various magazines such as *The Grocer's Assistant, The Graphic* and *The Lady's Pictorial. The Grocer's Assistant* said of Huntley & Palmers' 'Chivalry' (1912): '[it] will prove a splendid gift to friends of either sex.'

The war years brought a virtual halt to biscuit tin-box production. Only a few fairly simple tins with views of Belgian and French towns were made. Tins that had been made for the export market were instead sold to customers in Britain, and those which had not sold very well in previous years were promoted again.

Left: *Huntley & Palmers 'Roses',
1909, height 22 cm; 'Waterlilies',
1909, diameter 20.5 cm.
MacFarlane, Lang & Co 'Yule Log',
1910, diameter 13 cm.*

Below: *Huntley & Palmers
cardboard box for 'Roses', 1909
(flattened).*

Left: *Huntley & Palmers 'Chivalry',
1912, length 28 cm: the decoration
represents oxidised silver; 'Jewel
Case', 1913, width 19 cm: a plain
gold tin inside a wooden box,
covered in red-gilded cloth. Peek,
Frean & Co 'Mirror', c.1904,
diameter 11 cm: a mirror sits in the
lid of this tin. The pictures around
the sides are numbered and tell a
story.*

Right: *MacFarlane,
Lang & Co 'Lady's
Bag', 1909, width
12 cm. Huntley &
Palmers 'Forest',
1891, height 16 cm;
'Shell', 1912, width
19 cm.*

CWS Golden Bird 1920s, length 23.5 cm: this shape of tin was used extensively in the inter-war period for half-pound (228 gram) packets of biscuits. MacFarlane, Lang & Co 'Crinoline', 1932, height 21 cm; 'Peacock', 1931, width 17 cm. Wyllie, Barr & Ross Storks, c.1926, width 25 cm.

Tins 1919–1949

The years immediately after the First World War were quiet in terms of tin-box production. Political and economic instability, along with increased labour costs, led to a simplification in design when production got under way again in about 1919–20. More tins were made with illustrated paper labels. Coloured card covers were made for the standard paper-labelled tins and the biscuits themselves were sold in cellophane packets. At the same time as the Christmas tins were becoming simpler a new range of everyday tins with lithographed designs was produced. These tub-shaped tins were cheaper to make. This is not to say that no fancy tins were made, but whereas before the First World War ten or even twelve fancy tins per year was normal, in the inter-war period it was only two or three, supplemented by oval, round or square lithographed tins. The more simply shaped tins did not need boxes to protect them, so many tins were wrapped in cellophane.

MacFarlane, Lang & Co 'Oval Osborne', 1930s, height 14 cm; 'Large Water Biscuits' paper-labelled tin, c.1925, height 31 cm; 'Granola', 1930s, height 28.5 cm. Huntley & Palmers 'Wine Mixed', 1934, height 16 cm. Nairn's 'Abernethy Biscuits', 1930s, height 12 cm. (Front centre) McVitie & Price 'Inverness Shortbread', c.1935, length 17 cm.

In the 1920s and 1930s new leisure activities and increased freedom for women were reflected in the types of biscuits available. Various types of cocktail biscuits were produced which remained in vogue until the late 1960s. Foil-wrapped chocolate biscuits were introduced, which led to the use of large, flat tins so that the selection could be easily viewed when the lid was removed. Biscuit names evoked travel and glamour, such as 'Chocolate Berengaria' (an ocean liner) for a vanilla sandwich biscuit or 'Rialto' (cinemas) for a slightly sweet biscuit covered in plain chocolate.

The introduction of photolithography in the mid 1920s removed the stippled effect of the pre-war tins; the colours were brighter and had no shading. Photolithography meant that the designs did not have to be drawn on to the stones by hand but could be transferred photographically

Peek, Frean & Co Recreation, c.1937, width 24 cm. Huntley & Palmers 'Royal Scotch Shortbread', 1935, width 21 cm; 'Zodiac', 1937, width 21.5 cm; there are several cocktail recipes on the inside of the lid of this tin.

W. & R. Jacob & Co 'Dutch', 1936, width 11 cm. Huntley & Palmers 'Violets', c.1934, height 13.5 cm. CWS Dutch Barrel, c.1936, height 14 cm.

and then etched by hand. This was a development of an earlier process where the design had been put on the stone by a transfer.

Designs reflected public interests: there were many 'Old England' designs, paintings by famous artists decorated many rectangular tins, and country and garden scenes were always popular. Popular shapes included tea caddies, vases and 'tins' made from aluminium.

One of the main developments after the First World War was the production of tins as children's toys; there had been a few made in the Edwardian period, but, with Germany's economy in ruins, toy imports had dried up. Hudson Scott was one of the companies in a good position to take over the trade. A whole series of games and toys were produced throughout the 1920s, including boats, forts, racing games, draughts boards, cars, vans, trains and houses. Crawford's, in particular,

William Crawford & Sons 'Antique Tea Caddy', 1929, height 15 cm. MacFarlane, Lang & Co 'Biscuit Box', 1920s, height 18 cm. William Crawford & Sons 'Walnut Tea Caddy', 1937, height 17.5 cm (including handle).

(Back left) Bilsland Brothers Ltd 'Coronation Souvenir Tea Caddy', with box, 1953, height 16 cm. (Front) Huntley & Palmers Royal Wedding, 1947, diameter 13 cm: this tin is made of a mixture of aluminium and tinplate owing to a shortage of materials. (Right) Peek, Frean & Co Centenary Miniatures, 1957, widths 9.5 cm, 6 cm and 9.5 cm.

Above: *CWS Travellers Rest, 1930s, width 20.5 cm. Carr & Co 'Chariot Race' by Professor Alex Wagner, 1936, width 23.5 cm. William Crawford & Sons 'Pearl and Ivory Trinket Box', 1928, width 29 cm.*

Right: *Carr & Co 'Post Packet', 1926, width 18 cm. Huntley & Palmers 'Money Box', 1933, height 13.5 cm.*

Below: *William Crawford & Sons 'Wedgwood Casket', 1932, length 24 cm. Huntley & Palmers 'Rocket', c.1936, length 31 cm; 'Garden', c.1934, length 31 cm: these Huntley & Palmers tins were part of a large series issued throughout the 1930s.*

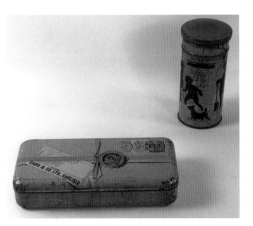

MacFarlane, Lang & Co 'Bramble', 1938, length 18 cm. Huntley & Palmers 'Tower of London', c.1937, length 20 cm. McVitie & Price 'Carnival', 1938, length 20 cm. Huntley & Palmers 'Rivoli', 1934, length 18 cm: the title of this tin refers to the biscuit selection inside. This shape was probably the most popular of the 1930s, used by many firms.

produced a lot of these.

Tins for Christmas 1939 had been produced before war was declared and sold because most people thought at first that the war would not last very long. However, production of fancy tins ceased at the beginning of 1940. A lot of the biscuits produced during the war went to the army as compo rations, packs of dry food to be consumed when fresh was not available. Large, green, square biscuit tins with pull-off lids were made for crates of rations. Each tin held $7^{1}/_{2}$ pounds (3.4 kg) of biscuits. Smaller tins went to the field kitchens.

Above: Huntley & Palmers 'Tribrek Motor Van', 1937, length 21 cm: this tin originally cost one shilling and sixpence.

In 1938 Peek, Frean & Co had made 224 different types of biscuit, but by 1942 this figure had dropped to less than forty. The same thing happened to all the biscuit manufacturers, with rationing, shortage of

Left: Marsh & Co Draughts Board, c.1926, width 20 cm. Huntley & Palmers 'FA Cup', 1926, height 21 cm: this 'tin' is made of aluminium by N. C. Joseph Ltd.

Huntley & Palmers 'Worcester Vase', 1934, height 26 cm. MacFarlane, Lang & Co 'Drum', 1939, height 13 cm: this originally had two drumsticks with it. Huntley & Palmers 'Italian Jar', 1927, height 18 cm (including handle); 'Holiday Haunts', 1926, height 19 cm. CWS Tea Caddy, c.1927, height 15 cm.

raw materials and war damage all leading to fewer varieties of biscuits being produced. This continued for some time after the war because sugar rationing was not lifted until 1954.

Shortage of materials also led to problems for the tin-box manufacturers after the war. The national debt led to a massive export drive, sponsored by the government, so that the few biscuit tins that were made were immediately sent overseas to even out the trade imbalance. It was far easier for customers in Singapore or the USA to buy British biscuits in fancy tins than it was for people in Britain, where it was almost impossible to get hold of them.The few tins that were produced tended to be small and often were made partially of aluminium. Most companies managed to produce tins to commemorate the wedding of Princess Elizabeth and Prince Philip in 1947.

Tins 1950–1980

It was the early 1950s before most manufacturers had found their feet again. Several of the smaller companies had not survived the Second World War and others had been taken over by multinationals. New shopping habits were changing the way the public bought biscuits: American-style supermarkets were introduced into Britain in the 1950s, and self-service became normal practice.

Some paper-labelled tins were still used, and the designs were the same as those used before the war. The shape of lithographed tins went through another simplification process, and round or square shapes

MacFarlane, Lang & Co Horses, c.1958, width 16 cm. Huntley & Palmers Harbour Scene by Vernon Ward, 1950s, width 23 cm.

Huntley & Palmers 'Cocktail Biscuits', c.1957, diameter 18 cm (back); Cupids, c.1953, width 23 cm (right). W. & R. Jacob & Co 'Fishing', c.1959, width 24cm (left).

Peek, Frean & Co 'Seashell', 1961, diameter 21 cm; Kemp's Budgerigar, c.1966, height 9 cm; Beatties Steamer, c.1960, width 26 cm.

Huntley & Palmers series of Iced Biscuits for children, 1950s–70s, diameter 13 cm: (clockwise from bottom left) 'William Tell', 1958; 'Muffin the Mule', c.1950; 'Peter Rabbit', c.1970; 'Noddy Cleans His Car', c.1966; 'Oswald the Ostrich', c.1951; (centre) 'Winnie the Pooh', c.1968. Some of the early tins in the series were made of aluminium.

Right: Weston's Biscuits Jazz, c.1964, height 10 cm. Huntley & Palmers 'Wedgwood', c.1965, height 18 cm. William Crawford & Sons National Dances, c.1960, height 9 cm.

Below: CWS 'Easter', c.1955, width 17 cm; 'Aquarium', c.1965, width 24 cm. (Huntley & Palmers also used this artwork in 1963.)

became standard. However, the quality of the artwork remained high throughout the 1950s, with similar themes to the 1930s prevailing and only the fashions changing. Works of art were still popular, as were sporting subjects and children's pictures. Television began to influence design in the early 1950s. Huntley & Palmers issued a series of tins

Peek, Frean & Co 'Stamps', c.1976, width 23 cm. Nabisco-Frears 'Cats', c.1972, width 22 cm. William Crawford & Sons 'Beatrix Potter Suitcase', c.1974, width 21 cm.

Peek, Frean & Co 'Snakes and Ladders', c.1977, width 20.5 cm; 'Playbox', c.1970, width 23 cm.

William Crawford & Sons 'Tartan Shortbread', c.1970, width 23 cm. Burton's Flowers, c.1974, height 10 cm. Scribans-Kemp/Barker & Dobson 'Writing Box', c.1975, width 18 cm; this was produced in conjunction with the Victoria and Albert Museum; it is a copy of an eighteenth-century writing box in the museum.

depicting children's television characters, and containing iced biscuits. The series continued into the 1970s. Flowers were popular, as were birds, and children with animals. Cocktail biscuits continued to be widely consumed, and American-style lithographed cans could be bought all year round. In the 1960s Huntley & Palmers began a series

*Carr & Co 'Treasure Island', c.1952, width 22 cm.
Huntley & Palmers 'Cocktail Snacks', 1967, width 15 cm;
'Elegance', 1963, width 16.5 cm;
'Cocktail Biscuits', c.1962, width 15 cm.*

of designs based on Wedgwood jasperware, some of which incorporated plastic handles.

By the 1960s photographs were appearing on tins. These were often of places, giving the tins a souvenir quality that the Victorian tins had had. Also by this time mechanisation had lowered the costs of manufacturing to the point where more complex designs could again be used. More often, though, it was the detail that enhanced the quality of the tin. Nostalgia for a golden age of advertising began to emerge in the 1970s, a trend which has continued up to the present day.

Huntley & Palmers 'Miniature tins' 1922–35 (some were reissued in the 1950s): (Back) Cubes all 4.5 cm high 'Littlefolk', 1922; 'Cheese Assorted', 1933; 'Rich Mixed', 1923; 'Nice', 1933; 'Cornish Wafers', c.1926; 'Thin Captain', c.1926, height 8.5 cm. (Centre) 'Ginger Nuts', 1933, length 6.5 cm; 'Dundee Cake', c.1933, diameter 5.5 cm; Rowntree's 'Chocolate Biscuits', c.1910, height 5 cm. (Front) Huntley & Palmers 'John Ginger', 1933, height 4.5 cm; 'Breakfast Biscuits', 1933, length 6.5 cm; 'Afternoon Tea', c.1922, length 7.5 cm.

Sample tins

Giving away biscuits as free samples was one of the most successful marketing strategies employed by the biscuit manufacturers and was used until the 1950s. The biscuits were given away when a new variety was launched or sales figures were low and needed a boost. All the national companies gave away free samples over the years. The tins were often just big enough to hold three or four biscuits. Bigger tins often held several different varieties, each individually wrapped in a greaseproof paper packet with the variety's name printed on it.

It is quite likely that each sample-tin design had a long life, and often the decoration was plain enough to be used for several different varieties of biscuit. Carr's used a red oblong tin for nearly twenty years. Some designs were based on the company's name in the current typographical style or were chosen from the stock catalogues of the tin-box manufacturers who designed prospectively for them. They often had small paper labels stuck on them, on which the name of the biscuit was written or printed. Some Huntley & Palmers' tins had a paper label on the base or, in the case of a major promotion, an advertisement printed on the bottom of the tin. Paper advertisements were sometimes stuck to the inside of the lid.

Crawford's had major sampling drives in the early years of the century and again in the 1930s at a time when most biscuit companies

William Crawford & Sons 'Trinket Box' sample tins, c.1928, (back) width 17 cm, (centre) width 10.5 cm, (front) diameter 8.5 cm; 'Tartan Shortbread', c.1930, width 11 cm; 'White Heather', c.1930, width 11 cm.

(Left to right, back to front) Huntley & Palmers Tub, c.1930, height 7 cm. 'Three biscuit' sample tins, all 8 cm diameter. Wyllie, Barr & Ross 'George V Silver Jubilee', 1935. McVitie & Price 'Mary, Queen of Scots', c.1935; Boy and Biscuit, c.1924; 'Edinburgh Castle', c.1938. William Crawford & Sons 'George VI Coronation', 1937; 'Rich Tea Biscuits', c.1932. W. & R. Jacob 'Water Biscuits', c.1933.

Gray, Dunn & Co sample tin, c.1910, width 10.5 cm. Huntley & Palmers 'Crest', c.1938, width 14.5 cm; blue soldered sample tin, c.1920, width 14.5 cm. W. & R. Jacob & Co blue tin c.1927, width 15.5 cm; red 'Cream Crackers', c.1925, width 15.5 cm; orange 'Cream Crackers', c.1930, width 18 cm. William Crawford & Sons 'Stork', c.1930, width 15 cm.

were retrenching. Small round tins containing three specially wrapped biscuits were delivered from door to door by 'hand sampling' teams, women employed on a temporary basis, or through the post to selected addresses. The delivery campaign was followed up by ensuring that the local grocer stocked the relevant biscuits. In the 1930s Crawford's not only targeted private families but also gave away large tins of free

Above: *William Crawford & Sons 'Abernethy', c.1938, width 10 cm. McVitie & Price Deer, c.1925, width 9.5 cm. Gray, Dunn & Co Thistle, c.1910, width 8.5 cm. Huntley & Palmers Biscuits, c.1926, width 8 cm. MacFarlane, Lang & Co 'Toasted Wheat', c.1934, width 8.5 cm; 'Granola', c.1910, width 8.5 cm. W. & R. Jacob & Co 'Trumpeter Assorted', c.1926, width 8 cm. Huntley & Palmers 'Crest' c.1938, width 7.5 cm. W. & R. Jacob & Co Biscuits, c.1903, width 8 cm. Peek, Frean & Co 'Golden Puffs', c.1910, width 8 cm. Hughes Biscuits, c.1924, width 9 cm. William Crawford & Sons 'Delightful Biscuits', c.1910, width 8.5 cm.*

Left: *MacFarlane, Lang & Co 'Cherry Blossom', 1920s, width 12 cm; this contained chocolate biscuits; paper-labelled sample tin, c.1925, height 20 cm; 'Gainsborough', 1931, height 15.5 cm; 'Turner Casket', 1935, width 15.5 cm (full-size versions of these two tins were available); cream tin with biscuit papers, 1920s, width 15.5 cm.*

Carr & Co 'Almond Crisps', c.1910, width 12 cm; 'Celebrated Biscuits', c.1900, width 12 cm. CWS 'Cream Crackers', c.1910, width 8 cm. Two Huntley & Palmers 'Mechanical Biscuits', c.1924, width 14.5 cm. Carr & Co 'Corn Cob', c.1910, width 12 cm. William Crawford & Sons Crest, c.1930, width 8 cm; 'Tartan Shortbread', c.1930, height 11 cm. Peek, Frean & Co 'Paper Packet', c.1900, width 9 cm.

samples at trade fairs to prospective customers. At the same time Crawford's were also producing the most fancy tins for Christmas, especially toys such as the 'Coach' in 1934 and the Mabel Lucie Attwell 'Fairy' tins of 1933-5.

McVitie & Price and the other Scottish companies used free samples extensively when they introduced shortbread to the English market in the first decade of the century. MacFarlane, Lang & Co's sample tins were sometimes small versions of their Christmas tins.

Jacob's and Huntley & Palmers issued miniature tins in the inter-war years. Jacob's were approximately 3 inches (7.5 cm) tall with two coloured sides advertising various biscuits. Huntley & Palmers' miniature tins were even smaller at $1^3/4$ inches (4.5 cm) tall and were decorated in imitation of the large shop display tins with the garter and buckle design. There were also rectangular tins and tubs of a similar size, some of which were re-issued in the 1950s. These tins were intended as children's stocking fillers. In the 1950s Peek, Frean & Co issued several small tins decorated with representations of the gold medals they had won at fairs and exhibitions over the years.

Further reading

Adam, James S. *A Fell Fine Baker: The Story of United Biscuits.* Hutchinson Benham Ltd, London, 1974.

Benson, John. *The Rise of Consumer Society in Britain 1880–1980.* Longman, 1994.

Birchall, Johnston. *Co-op: The People's Business.* Manchester University Press, 1994.

Corley, T.A.B. *Quaker Enterprise in Biscuits: Huntley & Palmers of Reading 1822–1972.* Hutchinson, 1972.

Davies, Alec. *Package and Print.* Faber & Faber, 1967.

Forster, Margaret. *Rich Desserts and Captain's Thins.* Chatto & Windus, 1997.

Franklin, M.J. *British Biscuit Tins 1868–1939.* New Cavendish, 1979.

Franklin, M.J. *British Biscuit Tins.* Victoria and Albert Museum, 1984.

Griffith, David. *Decorative Printed Tins: The Golden Age of Printed Tin Packaging.* Studio Vista, 1989.

Hindley, Diana and Geoffrey. *Advertising in Victorian England.* Wayland, 1972.

Hine, Thomas. *The Total Package.* Little Brown & Co, New York, 1995. The psychology of packaging.

Hornsby, Peter. *Decorated Biscuit Tins.* Schiffer, Pennsylvania, 1984.

Hudson, Graham. *The Victorian Printer.* Shire, 1996.

Opie, Robert. *The Art of the Label.* Chartwell Books Inc, New Jersey, 1987.

Opie, Robert. *Miller's Advertising Tins.* Miller's Publications Ltd, 1999.

Pugh, Peter. *A Clear and Simple Vision.* Cambridge Business Publishing, 1991.

Rafferty, Kevin A. *The Story of Hudson Scott & Sons: Metal Box, James Street, Carlisle.* Thurnham & Sons, Carlisle, 1998.

Reader, W. J. *Metal Box: A History.* Heinemann, 1976.

Huntley & Palmers 'Robin', 1963, width 12.5 cm; two 'Vintage', c.1976, width 12.5 cm: probably issued to celebrate the 150th anniversary of the company; 'London Bus', 1976, height 8.5 cm. Gray Dunn & Co Hunting, c.1979, height 9 cm.

Places to visit

Beamish, The North of England Open Air Museum, Beamish, County Durham DH9 0RG. Telephone: 01207 231811. Website: www.merlins.demon.co.uk/beamish

Buckley's Yesterday's World, 89–90 High Street, Battle, East Sussex TN33 0AQ. Telephone: 01424 774269. Website: www.yesterdaysworld.demon.co.uk (Museum of shops.)

How We Lived Then, 20 Cornfield Terrace, Eastbourne, East Sussex BN21 4NS. Telephone: 01323 737143. (Museum of shops.)

Manderston House, Duns, Berwickshire TD11 3PP. Telephone: 01361 883450. Website: www.manderston.demon.co.uk (Huntley & Palmers' tins.)

The Museum of Memories, Wigan Pier, Wallgate, Wigan, Lancashire WN3 4EU. Telephone: 01942 323666.

Museum of Reading, The Town Hall, Blagrave Street, Reading, Berkshire RG1 1QH. Telephone: 0118 939 9800. Website: www.reading.gov.uk/museum (Huntley & Palmers' tins.)

The Robert Opie Collection, Museum of Advertising and Packaging, Albert Warehouse, The Docks, Gloucester GL1 2EH. Telephone: 01452 302309.

The Shambles Museum, Church Street, Newent, Gloucestershire GL18 1PP. Telephone: 01531 822144. (Museum of Victorian life.)

York Castle Museum, Eye of York, York YO1 9RY. Telephone: 01904 613161. Website: www.york.gov.uk/heritage/museums/castle (Victorian street.)

The bottoms of tins were often as decorative as the upper surfaces. Huntley & Palmers 'Orient', 1887, length 24 cm. Peek Frean & Co 'Vineyard', 1903, length 25 cm: this tin has the original label with the name of the design; 'Dragon', 1895, height 15 cm.